10/15

W9-AZB-449

POWER UP!

A VISUAL EXPLORATION OF ENERGY

SHAKER PALEJA
ART BY GLENDA TSE

 annick press
toronto + new york + vancouver

Edited by Pam Robertson
Copyedited by Catherine Marjoribanks
Proofread by Linda Pruessen
Additional research and writing by Paula Ayer
Designed by Glenda Tse

Annick Press Ltd.

We acknowledge the support of the Canada Council for the Arts, the Ontario Arts Council, and the Government of Canada through the Canada Book Fund (CBF) for our publishing activities.

ONTARIO ARTS COUNCIL
CONSEIL DES ARTS DE L'ONTARIO
an Ontario government agency
un organisme du gouvernement de l'Ont.

Cataloging in Publication

Paleja, S. N. (Shaker Natvar), author
    Power up! : a visual exploration of energy / Shaker Paleja ; art by Glenda Tse.

Includes bibliographical references and index.
Issued in print and electronic formats.
ISBN 978-1-55451-726-8 (pbk.).—ISBN 978-1-55451-727-5 (bound).—
ISBN 978-1-55451-728-2 (html).—ISBN 978-1-55451-729-9 (pdf)

    1. Power resources—Juvenile literature. I. Tse, Glenda, 1991–, illustrator II. Title.

TJ163.23.P35 2015   J333.79   C2014-906627-9
                                                C2014-906628-7

Distributed in Canada by:
Firefly Books Ltd.
50 Staples Avenue, Unit 1
Richmond Hill, ON
L4B 0A7

Published in the U.S.A. by Annick Press (U.S.) Ltd.
Distributed in the U.S.A. by:
Firefly Books (U.S.) Inc.
P.O. Box 1338 Ellicott Station
Buffalo, NY 14205

Printed in China

Visit us at: www.annickpress.com
Visit Shaker Paleja at: shakerpaleja.com
Visit Glenda Tse at: glendatse.com

Also available in e-book format. Please visit www.annickpress.com/ebooks.html for more details. Or scan

TABLE OF CONTENTS

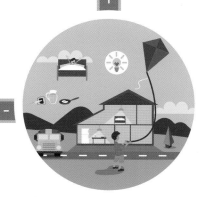

INTRODUCTION TO ENERGY

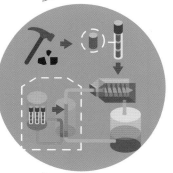

NON-RENEWABLE ENERGY

RENEWABLE ENERGY

THE FUTURE OF ENERGY

WHAT IS ENERGY?

THE WORD "ENERGY" CAN MEAN A LOT OF DIFFERENT THINGS.

Your body needs energy to get out of bed, walk, and even think.

Energy lights up your house and makes things work.

The food you eat for breakfast gives you energy.

The bus that takes you to school needs energy from fuel to make it go.

There's energy in sunlight and in the motion of wind and water.

ENERGY IS THE ABILITY TO DO WORK.

Energy can't be created or destroyed, but it can be transferred from one place or thing to another, or changed from one form to another. Your body does this every time it breaks down food into energy you can use.

Plants absorb energy from the sun and convert it into **chemical energy**, which is stored in the plant's molecules.

Your system breaks down food molecules to release energy, which you use any time you move. Any object that moves has **kinetic energy**, the energy of motion.

SOLAR ENERGY

CHEMICAL ENERGY

KINETIC ENERGY

WHAT DO WE USE ENERGY FOR? *US, 2012

Energy comes from many sources. We use it—in all its different forms—to make our lives easier and better.

BUSINESS: heating, cooling, and lighting for buildings where people work

INDUSTRY: energy for making, extracting, and refining things—like metals, wood, plastics, and glass

TRANSPORTATION: fuel for vehicles of all kinds

HOMES: heating, cooling, and lighting for buildings where people live

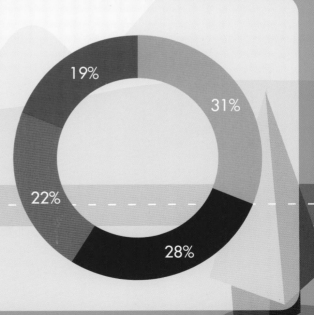

19%

31%

22%

28%

WHERE DOES ENERGY COME FROM?

SOLAR

The **sun** produces a huge amount of light and heat energy, only some of which eventually hits the earth. Solar panels or cells help us grab the sun's energy to use for heating, or to convert into **electricity.**

WIND

Wind comes from heat and pressure changes that occur when the sun warms the surface of the earth. Rotating machines called **turbines** can convert the kinetic energy of the wind's motion into electricity.

NUCLEAR

Nuclear energy comes from the power of atoms—tiny pieces of matter. When an atom of uranium is split, massive amounts of energy are released. This energy can be used to generate electricity.

GEOTHERMAL

Geothermal energy doesn't come from the sun. Instead, it comes from heat and steam deep within the earth. Geothermal energy can heat buildings or be converted into electricity.

BIOMASS

Biomass can be wood, grass, manure, corn, or even food scraps—all things that once absorbed the sun's energy to grow. It can be burned to produce heat and generate electricity, or turned into a liquid (biofuel) that can power vehicles.

HYDRO

The sun's heat creates the cycle of evaporation and rain that makes water flow. The movement of water through spinning turbines creates **hydroelectricity**. ("Hydro" means water, in Greek.)

ELECTRICITY

Electricity is called a "secondary" energy source. That's because it has to be generated from a "primary" energy source—like moving water, the sun's rays, wind, nuclear power, or fossil fuels—before being carried into houses and buildings to provide light and power.

The energy we use to make cars and buses go, light our houses, and power our devices comes from different places and things. But if you look back far enough, you'll see that most of it originally came from the power of the sun.

OIL   COAL   NATURAL GAS

1. Most of the energy that powers our vehicles and supplies our electricity comes from **fossil fuels.** Millions of years ago, even before dinosaurs, these fuels were living things—ancient plants and animals fed by energy from the sun's rays.

2. When these living things died, they were buried under layers of mud, sand, and rock. Heat, pressure, and bacteria helped them decompose. The sun's energy, stored inside them, became more and more concentrated.

3. Eventually, they were converted into **oil** (a thick black liquid, also called petroleum), **coal** (a black rock), and **natural gas** (a clear gas).

RENEWABLE ENERGY

You can't use up things like sun, wind, and water, because they're naturally replenished, or renewable. Different technologies can convert these natural types of energy into forms we can use.

SOLAR

WIND

HYDRO

BIOMASS

GEOTHERMAL

28.3 MILLION
PEOPLE WORLDWIDE USE HYDROPOWER

1.5 MILLION
US HOMES ARE POWERED BY BIOMASS

24 COUNTRIES USE GEOTHERMAL POWER

1 hour of sunlight (if we could capture it all) could power the world for **1 year**

300 homes can be powered by **1 wind turbine**

IS NUCLEAR ENERGY RENEWABLE?
DEPENDS WHO YOU ASK!

Yes. With better technology to find new sources of uranium and get it out of the ground, we'll have enough to last for the rest of time.

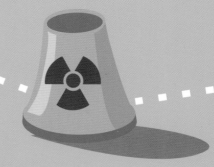

NON-RENEWABLE ENERGY

Fossil fuels take millions of years to form from ancient plant matter under the surface of the earth. When this kind of energy is used up, it's gone for good. That's why we call it non-renewable.

OIL

COAL

NATURAL GAS

HOW MUCH PLANT MATTER DOES IT TAKE TO PRODUCE FOSSIL FUELS?

WHAT'S OUR ENERGY MIX?

 FOSSIL FUEL

RENEWABLE

NUCLEAR

23 TONS

PREHISTORIC PLANT MATTER

=

1L (0.25 GALLONS)

GASOLINE

=

10 KM (6 MILES)

DISTANCE IN AN AVERAGE CAR

Oil that comes from the ground needs to be processed—or "refined"—to turn it into the gasoline that fills up cars. Three barrels of oil produces about two barrels of gasoline.

10 KG (22 LB) PREHISTORIC PLANT MATTER

=

1 KG (2.2 LB) COAL

=

ELECTRICITY TO POWER 8 LIGHT BULBS FOR 10 HOURS

1 YEAR'S WORTH OF PLANT GROWTH ON EARTH

=

AMOUNT OF FOSSIL FUEL USED WORLDWIDE IN 1 DAY

No. Nuclear energy comes from splitting uranium atoms, and there's a limited amount of uranium on earth.

83%
ENERGY SOURCES, US
9%
8%

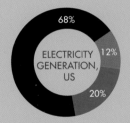
68%
ELECTRICITY GENERATION, US
12%
20%

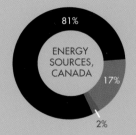
81%
ENERGY SOURCES, CANADA
17%
2%

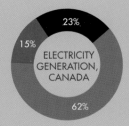
23%
15%
ELECTRICITY GENERATION, CANADA
62%

⚡ ELECTRICITY

US ENERGY CONSUMPTION (2012)

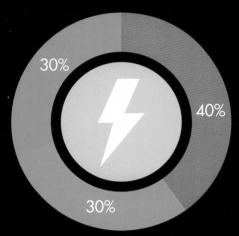

30%

40%

30%

 ELECTRICITY

 TRANSPORT

 OTHER

21% OF PEOPLE WORLDWIDE HAVE NO ACCESS TO ELECTRICITY

WHAT'S THE TOP SOURCE OF ELECTRICITY IN YOUR STATE/PROVINCE? *US, CANADA 2010

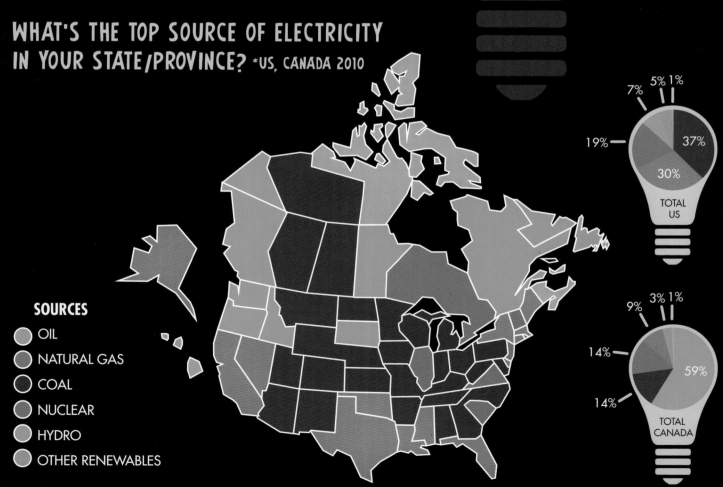

SOURCES
- OIL
- NATURAL GAS
- COAL
- NUCLEAR
- HYDRO
- OTHER RENEWABLES

TOTAL US

7% 5% 1%
19%
37%
30%

TOTAL CANADA

9% 3% 1%
14%
59%
14%

Electricity can be generated, or produced, from just about every energy source. Almost all of it comes from transferring a mechanical source of energy—usually a spinning turbine (like a big fan or propeller)—into electrical energy, with the help of a generator (a device kind of like a big electric motor).

HOW IS ELECTRICITY GENERATED?

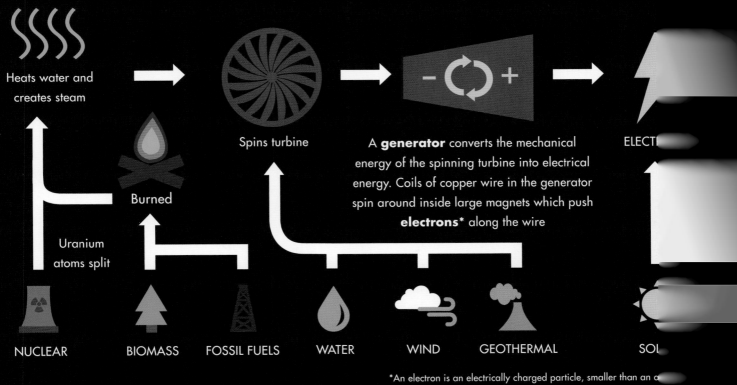

Heats water and creates steam

Spins turbine

A **generator** converts the mechanical energy of the spinning turbine into electrical energy. Coils of copper wire in the generator spin around inside large magnets which push **electrons*** along the wire

ELECTR

Burned

Uranium atoms split

NUCLEAR   BIOMASS   FOSSIL FUELS   WATER   WIND   GEOTHERMAL   SOL

*An electron is an electrically charged particle, smaller than an a
Moving electrons carry energy in the form of electricity.

THE POWER GRID

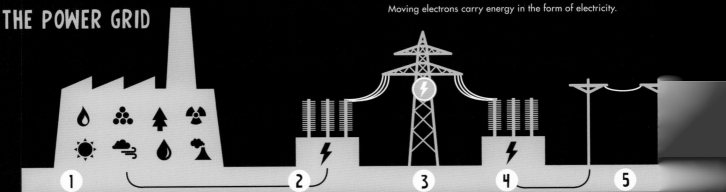

1 2 3 4 5

1 Electricity is generated in a power station.
2 It travels through wires to a switchyard, where a device called a transformer steps up the voltage (or pressure) so it can travel long distances.
3 It travels along transmission lines.
4 When the electricity gets closer to where it's needed, another transformer reduces the voltage again (otherwise it would blow out all your appliances!).
5 Finally, the electricity travels on smaller lines, underground or on poles.

A SHORT HISTORY OF ENERGY

4000 BCE
For transportation and farm labor, humans use the muscle power of **horses** and other animals.

900 CE
Persians invent **windmill** with rotating fabric sails, for grinding grain.

A REALLY LONG TIME AGO
The earliest humans—and all life on earth before them—use only the **sun's** energy, which gives them heat and light, and helps food grow.

For a long time, our energy needs are modest. We burn **biomass** (wood, dung, and straw) and gather small amounts of **coal, oil,** and **gas** that seep out of the ground to use for heat, cooking, and light.

2000 BCE
Coal first used in China for heating and cooking.

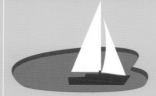

A MILLION YEARS AGO
Some genius discovers that rubbing two sticks together creates **fire**. This is huge! Now people can cook food to consume calories more efficiently (less raw food = less chewing), and produce heat and light even when the sun is down.

5000 BCE
Ancient Mesopotamians (and later, Egyptians) use **wind** power to sail the seas.

200 BCE
Greeks and Romans use **wind** and **water** wheels to power mills for grinding grain and pumping water.

1600—1700s
Cutting down **trees** to produce charcoal is a prime cause of European deforestation.

300 CE
First known **oil wells** drilled in China.

3500 BCE
In Asia and Europe, there is widespread use of **charcoal** (made from charred wood), which burns hotter than wood and makes metalworking possible.

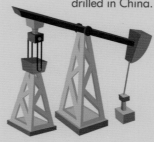

MID 1700s
Better mining and cooking techniques, combined with the invention of the coal-powered steam engine, help **coal** become the main fuel source in Europe, and drive the Industrial Revolution of the next century.

1850s
First North American oil wells drilled, in Ontario and Pennsylvania.

1948
World's largest **oil** field discovered, in Saudi Arabia.

1892
First use of underground **geothermal** energy to heat buildings, in Idaho.

1980s
Scientists first gather evidence that burning **fossil fuels** like oil and coal is contributing to global climate change.

1950
First **nuclear** power plants built, in the US and Russia.

1880–1950
Age of coal: coal replaces wood as top fuel source in the US.

1820s
First **natural gas** well drilled, in New York.

1890s
First cars powered by **gasoline,** derived from **oil.**

1970s
US **oil** production starts to drop, leading to more oil imported from other countries.

1900s
With the spread of **electricity** and the mass-produced automobile, energy use begins to double every 10 years.

1600–1800s
Starting in the 1600s, people hunt **whales** and use their oil to fuel lamps. By the end of the 1800s, some whale species are severely endangered. Fortunately **petroleum (oil)** is taking over as a fuel source.

1880s
First **electric** light; first **hydroelectric** plant generates power from water, in Wisconsin.

200b
Global **oil** production peaks at 70 billion barrels per day. Efforts to develop energy from alternative sources increase worldwide.

INTRODUCTION TO ENERGY   10

ENERGY TODAY

ENERGY SOURCES

 OIL   NATURAL GAS   COAL   RENEWABLE ENERGY   NUCLEAR

OIL 37%

- 🚗 71%
- 🏭 23%
- 🏠 5%
- 🔌 1%

NATURAL GAS 27%

- 🚗 3%
- 🏭 33%
- 🏠 28%
- 🔌 36%

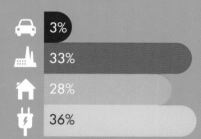

Of the fossil fuels, oil's top use is in vehicles, while most coal goes to generate electricity. Natural gas, a growing source of electricity, is also important for industry. It's used in homes to fuel gas furnaces, stoves, and water heaters.

COAL 18%

- 🚗 9%
- 🏭 <1%
- 🔌 91%

RENEWABLE ENERGY 9%

- 🚗 13%
- 🏭 25%
- 🏠 9%
- 🔌 53%

Over half of renewable energy—mostly from hydropower—goes to electricity production.

NUCLEAR 8%

- 🔌 100%

In North America today, most of our energy comes from fossil fuels, with smaller amounts from nuclear and renewables. On the left, you can see how much each energy source contributes to the total United States energy supply, and the share of that source that goes to various uses. On the right, you can see how our energy use breaks down.

ENERGY USES

TRANSPORTATION INDUSTRY RESIDENTIAL & COMMERCIAL ELECTRICITY

TRANSPORTATION 28%
93%
3%
4%

INDUSTRY 22%
40%
42%
7%
11%

Industry includes things like forestry, mining, oil refining, and chemical, metal, and glass manufacturing. If you factor in electricity, industry uses almost a third of the US energy supply.

RESIDENTIAL & COMMERCIAL 10%
17%
74%
1%
8%

ELECTRICITY 40%
1%
24%
41%
12%
21%

About a third of electricity in the US goes to homes, with another third going to commercial use (like offices, shops, hospitals, and stadiums), and the last third to industry.

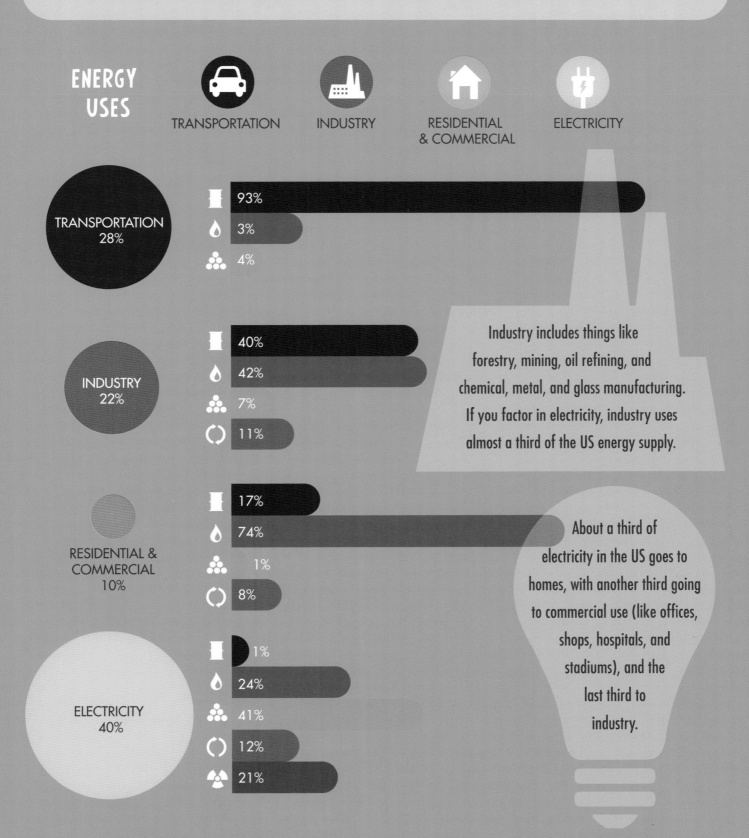

EMISSIONS

GREENHOUSE GASES (GHGs)

Greenhouse gases—mostly carbon dioxide, methane, and nitrous oxide—are all found naturally in the earth's atmosphere. But human activities, especially burning fossil fuels for energy, are producing more and more of them.

HOW LONG CAN GHGs STAY IN THE ATMOSPHERE?

The impact of greenhouse gases depends on how long they stay in the atmosphere before breaking down. Some GHGs stay in the atmosphere longer than others.

CO_2 1,000 YEARS +

CH_4 12 YEARS

N_2O 114 YEARS

GWP (OVER 100 YEARS)

Certain gases absorb more heat than others, so they contribute more to warming the planet. Global Warming Potential (GWP) is a measure of how much a greenhouse gas contributes to global warming per pound, compared to CO_2.

CO_2 1

CH_4 21

N_2O 310

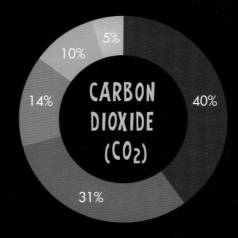

CARBON DIOXIDE (CO_2)

5%
10%
14%
40%
31%

You emit CO_2 every time you breathe, and plants and trees pull it out of the air so they can grow. But the burning of fossil fuels is creating more CO_2 than our planet can handle, and global deforestation means there are fewer and fewer trees to do the job of cleaning it up.

WHICH ACTIVITIES PRODUCE THE MOST CO_2?

- Burning fossil fuels to generate electricity
- Combustion of fossil fuels in transportation
- Industry (fossil fuel combustion, metal and chemical production, etc.)
- Homes and businesses (non-electrical heating, cooking, etc.)
- Other

Fossil fuels supply a huge portion of our energy in the US and Canada. But oil, coal, and natural gas need to be combusted (or burned) to generate electricity or make vehicles go. During this process, they release substances called greenhouse gases into the air, which can have big side effects for our planet, and for us.

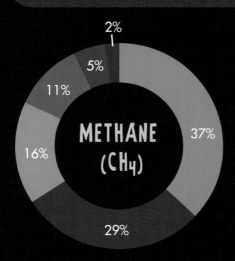

METHANE (CH4)

2%
5%
11%
16%
29%
37%

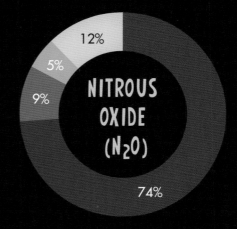

NITROUS OXIDE (N2O)

12%
5%
9%
74%

Natural gas is partly made up of methane, so extracting gas from the ground releases methane into the atmosphere. Since natural gas is often found near oil deposits, oil production also releases methane. Other sources are agriculture (from animals' digestive gas and manure) and landfills, which produce methane as waste decomposes.

Nitrous oxide is a naturally occurring element, but about two-fifths of N_2O in the atmosphere today comes from human activities. N_2O is a big concern. It absorbs even more heat than CO_2 so contributes more per pound to global warming.

WHICH ACTIVITIES PRODUCE THE MOST CH4?

● Natural gas and oil production

● Agriculture

● Landfills

● Coal mining

● Other

● Waste treatment

WHICH ACTIVITIES PRODUCE THE MOST N2O?

● Agriculture

● Industry (producing plant fertilizers and synthetic fabrics)

● Transportation

● Other

CLIMATE EFFECTS

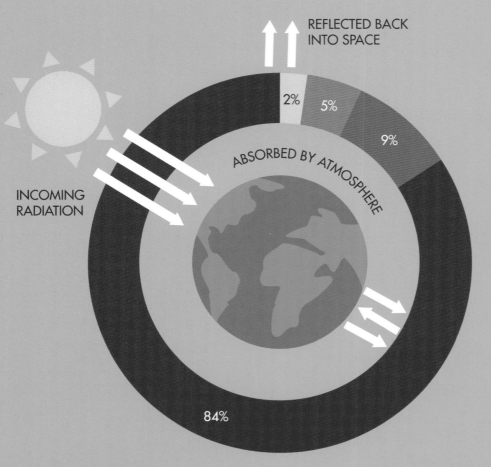

REFLECTED BACK
INTO SPACE

2%   5%

9%

ABSORBED BY ATMOSPHERE

INCOMING
RADIATION

84%

When sunlight hits the earth,
some of it bounces back into
space through our atmosphere.
GHGs trap this heat, making
the earth's atmosphere act like
a "greenhouse." Over time,
the temperature of the earth
becomes warmer.

BREAKDOWN OF GHGs PRODUCED BY HUMAN ACTIVITY

● Carbon Dioxide (CO_2)

● Methane (CH_4)

● Nitrous Oxide (N_2O)

● Other (Fluorinated Gases)

CHANGE IN GLOBAL GHG LEVELS FROM YEAR 0 TO 2000

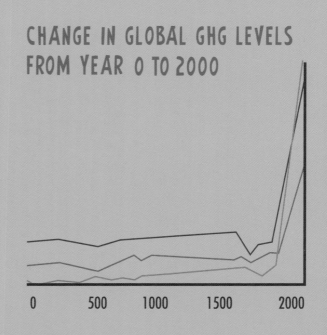

0   500   1000   1500   2000

Greenhouse gases trap heat in the earth's atmosphere, making the planet hotter. As emissions increase, this causes changes to our climate—the pattern of weather over time.

WHAT DOES CLIMATE CHANGE MEAN?

 Changes in the weather

More floods, droughts, and storms

 More heat waves

 Warming oceans and rising sea levels

EFFECTS OF CLIMATE CHANGE

 Affects food supply

 Alters ecosystems

 Threatens animal species

 Threatens water supply and quality

 Harms human health and safety

COUNTRIES WITH HIGHEST CO₂ EMISSIONS AND PER-PERSON EMISSIONS (2011)

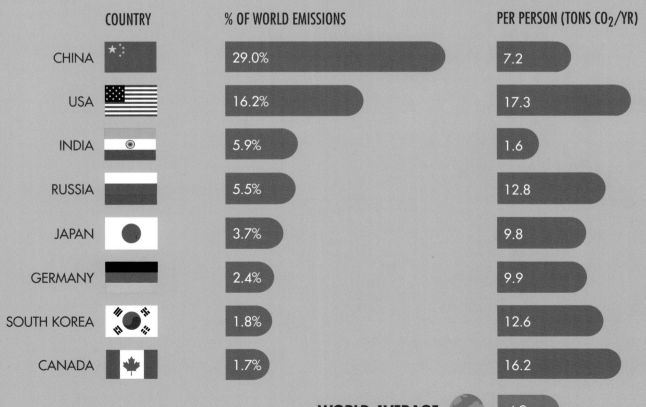

COUNTRY	% OF WORLD EMISSIONS	PER PERSON (TONS CO₂/YR)
CHINA	29.0%	7.2
USA	16.2%	17.3
INDIA	5.9%	1.6
RUSSIA	5.5%	12.8
JAPAN	3.7%	9.8
GERMANY	2.4%	9.9
SOUTH KOREA	1.8%	12.6
CANADA	1.7%	16.2
WORLD AVERAGE		4.9

OIL

WHAT IS IT?

Oil is a fossil fuel, and the most used source of energy for transportation.

HOW DO WE GET OIL?

% OF OIL FROM EACH PROCESS

10% **Primary Recovery**
The easiest oil to reach is the black liquid that spurts from the ground and up through pipes once a well has been drilled, because of pressure from gases underneath.

30% **Secondary Recovery**
When that oil is gone, water or gases are pumped into the ground, creating pressure that forces the deeper oil to the surface.

60% **Tertiary Recovery**
The oil that's left is thicker, heavier, and harder to get. In the past, oil companies often left it underground. Today it can be reached by injecting steam or chemicals.

TOP 4 OIL-CONSUMING COUNTRIES
(IN MILLION BARRELS/DAY)

● OIL PRODUCED   ● OIL IMPORTED

US   11.1   7.5

CHINA   4.4   5.9

JAPAN   0.4/4.6

INDIA   0.9/2.7

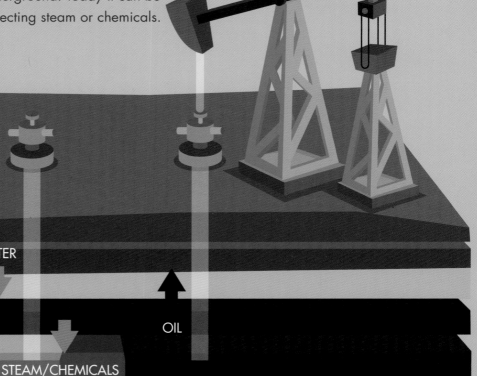

WATER

OIL

OIL

STEAM/CHEMICALS

HOW MUCH OIL USED IN THE US IS IMPORTED?

- 1950 **8%**
- 2003 **56%**
- 2012 **40%**

The United States uses more oil than it produces, so it has to import some from other countries. Some people think depending on "foreign" oil is risky because forces beyond a country's control—like a change in leadership or transportation issues—could disrupt the flow.

TOP SUPPLIERS OF OIL TO US
(IN MILLION BARRELS/DAY)

Over 80% of US oil imports come from 5 countries.

2.5	1.3	0.8	0.7	0.4
CANADA	SAUDI ARABIA	MEXICO	VENEZUELA	IRAQ

ENERGY FROM OIL

34% GLOBAL   **40%** US   **32%** CANADA

WHO HAS THE OIL?

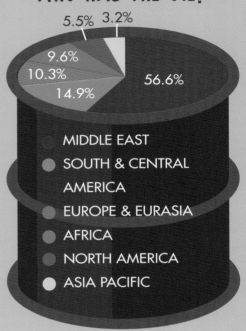

- 56.6%
- 14.9%
- 10.3%
- 9.6%
- 5.5%
- 3.2%

- MIDDLE EAST
- SOUTH & CENTRAL AMERICA
- EUROPE & EURASIA
- AFRICA
- NORTH AMERICA
- ASIA PACIFIC

ENERGY IN, ENERGY OUT

Oil supplies energy, but finding and producing it also uses energy at every stage:

| Exploring for oil and developing new reserves | Bringing oil to the surface | Refining oil so it can be transported and used | Transporting oil by trains, trucks, or ships | Building pipelines to transport oil over long distances |

PROS

- ✔ Plentiful (for now)
- ✔ Technology to use it already exists
- ✔ Most powerful source for moving vehicles
- ✔ Creates jobs and wealth

CONS

- ✘ Burning it produces greenhouse gases
- ✘ Production and transport is expensive and energy-intensive
- ✘ Potential for dangerous spills and accidents
- ✘ Some has to be imported to the US

NATURAL GAS

WHAT IS IT?

Natural gas is a fossil fuel found in rock formations underground. It's used to generate electricity and as a fuel for gas furnaces, fireplaces, and stoves.

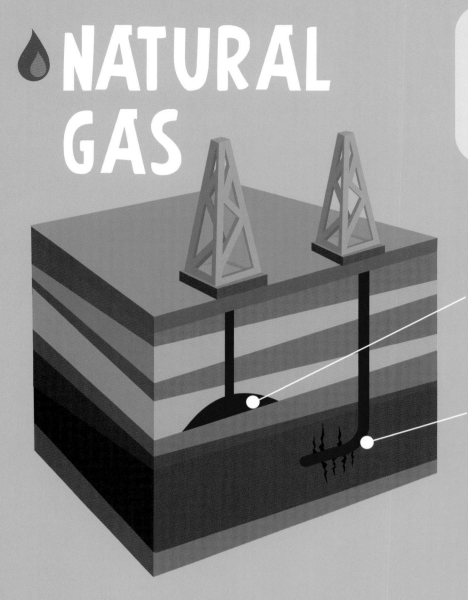

CONVENTIONAL AND UNCONVENTIONAL SOURCES OF NATURAL GAS

Conventional gas is found in gas fields, either on its own or next to oil deposits. It's extracted by drilling, just like oil, and is piped to where it's needed.

Shale gas, an unconventional source, is trapped in rock formations deep under the ground. Until recently, the technology didn't exist to get it out. Now shale is a growing source of natural gas in the United States, and it's also being used in Canada and China.

HOW IS SHALE GAS EXTRACTED?

Fracking, or hydraulic fracturing, involves blasting the rock with a pressurized liquid chemical mixture. The gas is released through the resulting cracks. Today, 95% of the natural gas used in the United States is produced in the United States.

TOP STATES PRODUCING SHALE GAS

- Pennsylvania
- West Virginia
- Louisiana
- Texas
- Arkansas

PERCENTAGE OF NATURAL GAS USED IN THE US THAT COMES FROM SHALE

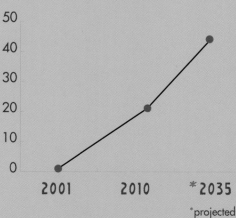

*projected

WHERE'S THE GAS?

- ● MIDDLE EAST
- ● EUROPE & EURASIA
- ● ASIA PACIFIC
- ● AFRICA
- ● NORTH AMERICA
- ● SOUTH & CENTRAL AMERICA

4.9% 4.3%
7.9%
8.7%
40.6%
33.7%

ENERGY FROM NATURAL GAS

24% GLOBAL   25% US   22% CANADA

Natural gas can be either compressed (compressed natural gas, or CNG) or supercooled to convert it into a liquid (liquefied natural gas, or LNG). These techniques make it easier to transport through pipelines and in tanker trucks.

LNG or CNG can be used instead of gasoline to fuel trucks and buses.

When it gets to where it's needed, LNG can be converted back into a gas for use in homes and buildings

ESTIMATED CARBON EMISSIONS OF FOSSIL FUELS*

Natural Gas (Conventional) — 203
Natural Gas (Shale) — 226
Liquefied Natural Gas — 250
Coal — 958

*In grams of CO_2 per kilowatt-hour of energy.

PROS

- ✔ Clean-burning compared to coal and oil
- ✔ Versatile energy source
- ✔ Abundant supply in US and Canada
- ✔ Industry employs over 1 million people

CONS

- ✘ Produces some CO_2
- ✘ Risk of explosions
- ✘ Sources are concentrated in a few places; has to be transported long distances
- ✘ Fracking for shale gas comes with environmental and health risks

 # COAL

WHAT IS IT?

Coal, a fossil fuel, is a black rock found underground. It's burned to generate a big part of the US electricity supply and to produce heat.

WHERE'S THE COAL?

- EUROPE & EURASIA
- ASIA PACIFIC
- NORTH AMERICA
- AFRICA
- SOUTH & CENTRAL AMERICA
- MIDDLE EAST

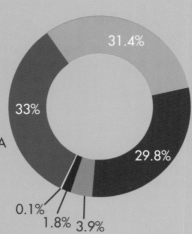

31.4%

33%

29.8%

0.1% 1.8% 3.9%

TOP COAL-CONSUMING COUNTRIES

- CHINA
- US
- INDIA
- REST OF WORLD

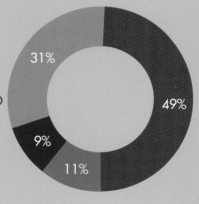

31%

49%

9%

11%

HOW DO WE GET COAL?

Surface mining: When coal is close to the surface, the top layer of earth is removed, usually with explosives, to create a large pit.

One type of surface mining is known as **mountaintop removal mining**. A summit or ridge of a mountain is removed to reach coal deposits underneath. This method is commonly used in the Appalachian Mountains of the eastern United States.

Underground mining: For coal found deeper underground, mines and tunnels are dug into the earth so the coal can be retrieved.

Machines scrape out or drill the coal from the ground and break it into pieces.

The coal is carried on large trucks or conveyors to a power plant where it's burned to produce electricity, or to factories where it's used by industry.

COAL SHAFT

MINE SHAFT

EFFECTS OF MOUNTAINTOP REMOVAL MINING

 Cheaper, requires less labor, and safer for workers than underground mining

 Significantly changes the landscape

 Deforestation

 Toxic chemicals associated with mining end up in ground, air, and water

 Pollution from mining chemicals is linked to lung cancer and other diseases

ENERGY FROM COAL

Coal produces 40 percent of all the world's electricity—and almost 40 percent of global CO_2 emissions! That's why many countries are trying to replace electricity from coal with cleaner alternatives.

CLEAN COAL?

Burning coal produces more CO_2 than any other energy source, as well as toxic metals that can end up in the air or water.

A technique called carbon capture and storage (CCS) pumps the CO_2 underground or under the ocean to reduce emissions into the air.

Coal can also be converted into a gas, which reduces CO_2 emissions.

PROS
- ✓ New CCS technology promises to reduce CO_2 impact
- ✓ Plenty of supply in US
- ✓ Efficient energy source
- ✓ Cheap

CONS
- ✗ Burning produces high CO_2 emissions and toxic ash
- ✗ Mining is harmful to environment and human health
- ✗ Risk of mining accidents
- ✗ Expensive to transport

NUCLEAR

HOW IS NUCLEAR ENERGY PRODUCED?

1 Uranium, a metallic element, is mined from the ground.

2 The uranium is made into pellets, which are lined up in fuel rods.

3 The rods are placed inside a nuclear reactor, and the uranium atoms are hit with particles called neutrons. This forces the atoms to split and causes a nuclear reaction.

4 The heat created by the reaction turns water to steam, which is used to generate electricity.

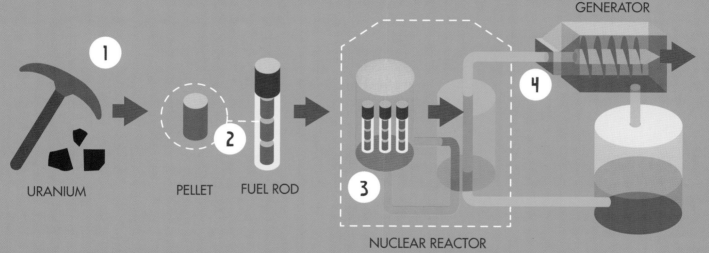

GENERATOR

URANIUM   PELLET   FUEL ROD   NUCLEAR REACTOR

NUCLEAR ENERGY PRODUCTION THROUGHOUT THE WORLD

● SHARE OF TOTAL ELECTRICITY   ● NUMBER OF REACTORS

COMPARISON OF POWER GENERATED FROM VARIOUS ENERGY SOURCES

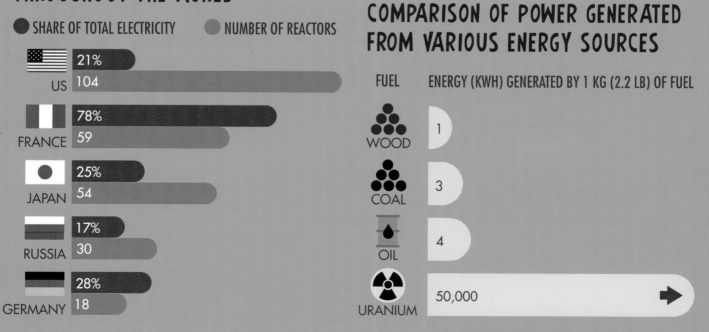

US — 21% — 104

FRANCE — 78% — 59

JAPAN — 25% — 54

RUSSIA — 17% — 30

GERMANY — 28% — 18

FUEL   ENERGY (KWH) GENERATED BY 1 KG (2.2 LB) OF FUEL

WOOD — 1

COAL — 3

OIL — 4

URANIUM — 50,000

WHERE DOES NUCLEAR WASTE GO?

Nuclear energy produces none of the greenhouse gases that come with burning fossil fuels. But the used fuel does create nuclear waste, which can stay radioactive for thousands of years and must be stored safely. Nuclear waste can be stored in three ways.

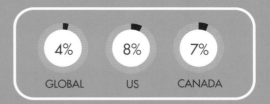

4%
GLOBAL

8%
US

7%
CANADA

 Storage chamber at the nuclear reactor site

 Temporary disposal site in an unpopulated area, like one proposed at Yucca Mountain in Nevada

 Recycled into medical isotopes to treat diseases

MAJOR NUCLEAR ACCIDENTS

Accidents at nuclear power plants, or during transportation of uranium fuel or waste, can be catastrophic, releasing dangerous and potentially deadly radioactivity into the environment.

1986: CHERNOBYL, UKRAINE
CAUSE: Explosion and fire at plant
EFFECTS: 56 people killed; estimated 4,000 deaths from cancer caused by radiation exposure; several cities abandoned

1979: THREE MILE ISLAND, PENNSYLVANIA, US
CAUSE: Design and operator errors
EFFECTS: Cleanup cost of $1 billion; increase in cancer cases in the area; sparked new nuclear safety rules in the US

2011: FUKUSHIMA, JAPAN
CAUSE: Plant hit by tsunami after earthquake
EFFECTS: 300,000 people evacuated, 37 injured; cleanup of ocean water contaminated with radiation expected to take decades

PROS

- ✔ Fuel produces no CO_2 or pollution
- ✔ Waste can be reduced through recycling
- ✔ Nuclear plants have low operating costs
- ✔ Huge capacity for generating energy
- ✔ Technology to use it already exists

CONS

- ✘ Mining, refining, and transportation of uranium use energy and produce GHGs
- ✘ Produces nuclear waste
- ✘ Plants are expensive and time-consuming to build
- ✘ Risk of dangerous accidents
- ✘ Health and environmental risks from uranium exposure

UNCONVENTIONAL OIL SOURCES

WHAT ARE THEY?

Our planet has lots of oil, but we're quickly using up the "conventional" oil that's easy to access. If we keep using oil at the rate we are now, we will have to turn increasingly to sources that are much harder to find. Most of the oil we have left is in hard-to-reach places, or in forms that are tough to extract and use.

MORE CARS, MORE OIL

There are about **3 vehicles** for every **4 people** in the US.

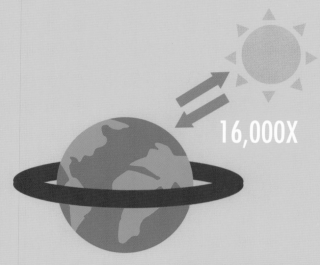

16,000X

In 2010, **vehicles** in the US **traveled almost 5 trillion km** (3 trillion miles)—the equivalent of going to the sun and back 16,000 times.

HOW DOES OIL CONTRIBUTE TO GREENHOUSE GAS EMISSIONS?

20%

80%

● PRODUCING AND REFINING OIL
● VEHICLES BURNING GASOLINE

THE HIGH COST OF UNCONVENTIONAL OIL

It takes 1 barrel of oil to find and produce:

100

barrels conventional oil, **1990**

25

barrels conventional oil, **TODAY**

3

barrels unconventional oil, **TODAY**

OIL SANDS

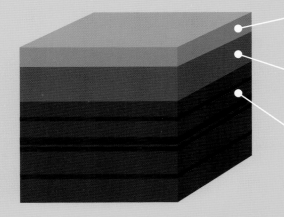

Light crude oil that flows easily is considered the best kind, because it's easy to get from the ground and convert into gasoline for cars.

Heavy oil, which is thicker, takes more energy to extract and convert.

The heaviest form of oil is **bitumen**, a very thick, sticky black oil trapped in layers of sand. The deposits where it's found are called oil sands, tar sands, or bituminous sands.

SLOW FLOW

Bitumen is so heavy it doesn't flow unless it's heated or mixed with something else. It takes a lot of energy, water, and other resources to get it out of the ground and separate the oil from the sand to make it usable.

2 TONS OF OIL SAND   4.5 BARRELS OF WATER   1 BARREL OF OIL

One technique for extracting bitumen, steam-assisted gravity drainage—which uses steam heat to make the bitumen liquid enough to flow—allows over 90% of the water used to be recycled.

Alberta, Canada, has two-thirds of the world's oil sands. Other countries with big oil sands deposits: Kazakhstan, Russia, and Venezuela.

ENVIRONMENTAL IMPACT OF OIL SANDS

3X Production and refining creates 3 times the CO_2 emissions compared with conventional oil

 Air pollution from heated bitumen and other chemicals, which can have health effects

Contamination of water with heavy metals and chemicals

 Clearing forest and removing topsoil

Alberta's oil sands are projected to last less than 160 years. Less than 50% of tar sands oil can be recovered using today's technology.

OFFSHORE DRILLING

Oceans cover about 70 percent of the earth's surface, so it's not surprising that a lot of our planet's oil reserves are found underwater. It's harder and more expensive to access this oil, but as oil supplies on land become scarcer, offshore drilling is becoming more common.

OIL RIGS

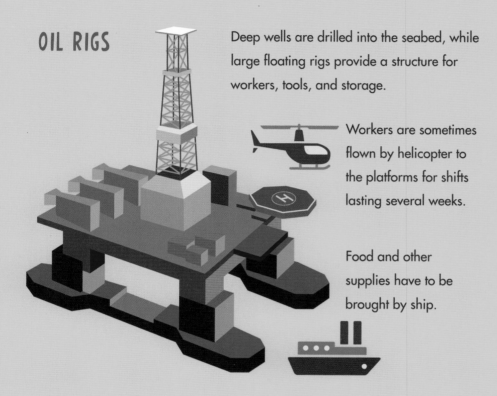

Deep wells are drilled into the seabed, while large floating rigs provide a structure for workers, tools, and storage.

Workers are sometimes flown by helicopter to the platforms for shifts lasting several weeks.

Food and other supplies have to be brought by ship.

NUMBER OF ULTRA-DEEP OFFSHORE WELLS
(IN WATER 1.5–2.5 KM/ 1–1.5 MILES DEEP)

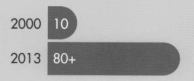

2000 10
2013 80+

MONEY SPENT ON OFFSHORE DRILLING
($ = $5 BILLION USD)

2002 $
2014 $$$$$$$

Oil spills are a major environmental hazard of offshore drilling. In 2010, an explosion on the Deepwater Horizon drilling station in the Gulf of Mexico caused it to sink, creating the biggest oil spill in US history.

IMPACT OF DEEPWATER HORIZON SPILL

4.9 million barrels of oil spilled

11 workers killed

Cost of cleanup: $14 billion

Affected area of ocean the size of Oklahoma

Over 8,000 animal species affected

OIL SHALE

Oil shale is sedimentary rock containing oil deposits. Processes that heat the rock or treat it with chemicals are used to extract shale oil, also called tight oil.

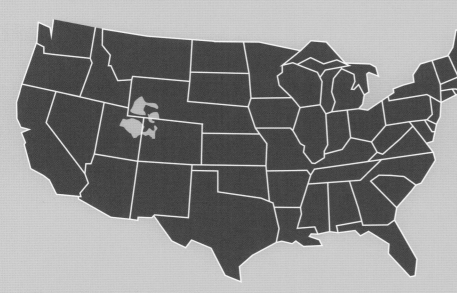

SHALE IN THE US

Over 62 percent of the world's shale oil deposits are in the United States, mostly in Colorado, Utah, and Wyoming.

WORLD OIL RESOURCES
(IN TRILLION BARRELS)

SHALE OIL 4.8

CONVENTIONAL OIL 1.3

The world has much more shale oil than conventional oil, but we don't yet have the technology to recover all of it.

The processes involved in mining and extracting shale oil can release CO_2, change the landscape, and produce waste that pollutes air and water. Mining shale oil from underground is usually less harmful to the environment than surface mining.

UNCONVENTIONAL OIL PROS AND CONS

✔ Domestic supply in Canada and the US reduces reliance on foreign oil

✔ New technologies can reduce environmental impact of unconventional oil

✔ Creates jobs and wealth in Canada and the US

✘ More expensive and energy-intensive to produce than conventional oil

✘ Greater environmental impact than conventional oil

✘ Risk of accidents and spills

3

☀ SOLAR

WHAT IS IT?

The sun's energy can be used in a couple of different ways. It can be captured by solar collectors and used for heat, or converted into electricity by devices called photovoltaic cells.

HOW DOES THE SUN PROVIDE ENERGY?

1 The super-hot core of the sun creates intense pressure as gravity pulls mass inward, forcing hydrogen and helium atoms together in nuclear fusion reactions. These reactions create huge amounts of energy, only some of which eventually reach earth.

2 **Solar collectors,** which can come in many different forms, including flat panels, towers, and tubes, are devices that absorb radiation from the sun. They transfer that energy to use for space heating, or to heat water for homes or industries.

3 Photovoltaic cells are small, flat electrical devices that convert energy from sunlight into electricity. **Solar panels**, which can go on rooftops, are composed of rows of photovoltaic cells.

4 Homes powered by solar energy can be connected to a larger electricity grid. Extra electricity produced during the day goes into the grid. At night, when the sun's not shining, the grid provides electricity the home needs.

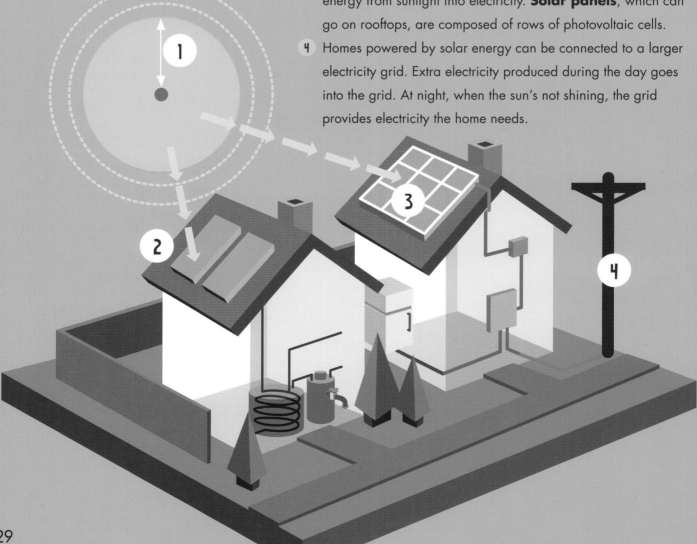

SOLAR GROWTH

Solar power is a growing source of electricity, and by 2050 it's projected to contribute 11 percent of the global supply.

- OFF GRID
- UTILITIES
- BUSINESSES
- HOMES

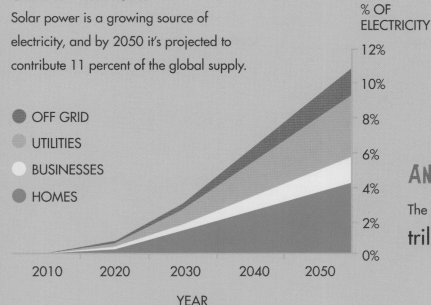

% OF ELECTRICITY

12%
10%
8%
6%
4%
2%
0%

2010 2020 2030 2040 2050

YEAR

ENERGY FROM SOLAR

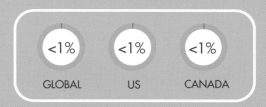

| <1% | <1% | <1% |
| GLOBAL | US | CANADA |

AN ENERGY POWERHOUSE!

The sun produces nearly **400 trillion trillion** watts of power *per second!*

TOP 5 COUNTRIES USING SOLAR POWER

- Germany
- Spain
- Japan
- US
- Italy

If it could all be captured and used, the energy in an area of sunny Nevada about the size of 50 football fields could supply enough electricity for all of the United States.

ON AND OFF

The sun is an intermittent energy source, which means the energy it produces stops and starts. You can't get energy from the sun at night, or when it's cloudy. But new technology is making it easier to store solar energy for later use.

PROS

- ✔ Environmentally friendly power source
- ✔ Unlimited supply
- ✔ Good energy source in developing countries
- ✔ Low operating costs once system is installed
- ✔ Can be used on a small or medium scale

CONS

- ✘ Manufacturing, transporting, and installing solar panels produces GHG emissions
- ✘ Must be stored to use when the sun isn't shining
- ✘ Only practical to use in sunny places
- ✘ High construction and installation costs
- ✘ More progress is needed to make the technology usable on a large scale

WIND

WHAT IS IT?
Wind currents propel the motion of large turbines. Their kinetic energy is then converted into electricity.

WHAT'S OUR WIND POTENTIAL?
in MW (megawatts) of power

2011: 237,699
2015: 397,859
2020: 586,729
2030: 917,798

TOP US STATES GENERATING ELECTRICITY FROM WIND POWER*

State	Percentage
IOWA	27%
SOUTH DAKOTA	26%
KANSAS	19%
IDAHO	16%
MINNESOTA	16%
NORTH DAKOTA	16%

*Percentage of total state electricity generation from wind power

HOW DOES WIND POWER WORK?
Wind farms are groups of wind turbines, which are large, spinning devices that convert the kinetic energy of wind into electricity.

1. Wind makes the blades of the turbine spin.
2. Inside the turbine, the blades make a rotor spin, and a generator converts the energy created by the spinning motion into electricity.
3. Electricity travels through transmission lines to homes and other buildings, where it's used.

US GOVERNMENT SUPPORT TO ENERGY INDUSTRIES (IN MILLION $/YEAR)

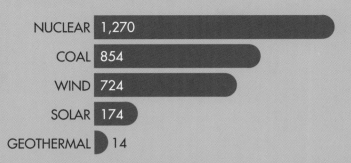

NUCLEAR	1,270
COAL	854
WIND	724
SOLAR	174
GEOTHERMAL	14

ENERGY FROM WIND

<1%	1.8%	<1%
GLOBAL	US	CANADA

TOP 10 COUNTRIES PRODUCING ELECTRICITY FROM WIND POWER   ENERGY IN TERAWATT-HOURS (TWH)

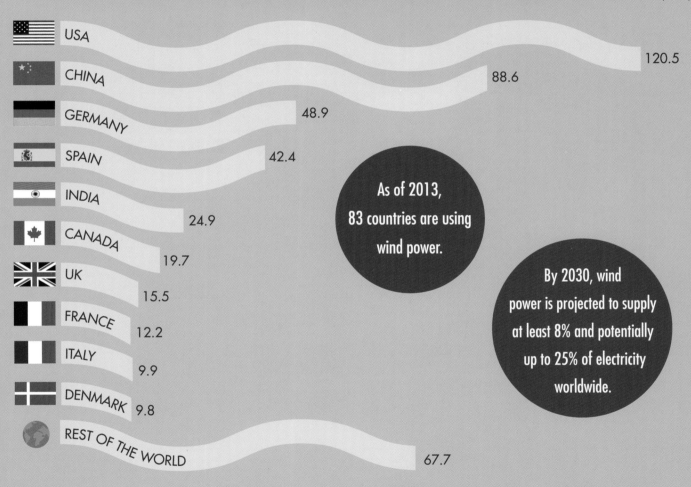

USA — 120.5
CHINA — 88.6
GERMANY — 48.9
SPAIN — 42.4
INDIA — 24.9
CANADA — 19.7
UK — 15.5
FRANCE — 12.2
ITALY — 9.9
DENMARK — 9.8
REST OF THE WORLD — 67.7

As of 2013, 83 countries are using wind power.

By 2030, wind power is projected to supply at least 8% and potentially up to 25% of electricity worldwide.

PROS

- ✔ No pollution or CO_2 emissions
- ✔ Unlimited supply
- ✔ Domestic source in US and Canada
- ✔ Low cost to operate; no fuel costs
- ✔ Farms can be built offshore, so no land is used

CONS

- ✘ Intermittent, unpredictable energy source
- ✘ No practical way to store energy
- ✘ Turbines kill some birds and bats
- ✘ Turbines produce noise in a constant, low hum
- ✘ Wind farms use lots of land and change the natural scenery

HYDRO

WHAT IS IT?

A major source of electricity, hydroelectric power is generated by the force of water flowing through dams.

HOW DOES HYDROELECTRICITY WORK?

1. A dam is built along a river, interrupting the water flow.
2. Water builds up behind the dam. As it falls downward, it creates pressure.
3. The pressure spins a turbine attached to a generator, which generates electricity.
4. Electricity travels along power lines to where it's needed.

China produces 32% of the world's hydroelectricity.

TOP HYDRO PRODUCERS (2011)

Hydroelectric production per year, in terawatt-hours
(1 TW = 1 trillion watts)

Country	Production
CHINA	691
CANADA	424
BRAZIL	372
US	319
RUSSIA	164

NUMBER OF HYDROELECTRIC POWER PLANTS

WORLDWIDE	48,000
US	2,000
CANADA	10,000

ELECTRICITY GENERATED FROM HYDRO (IN TWH)

ENERGY FROM HYDRO

6% GLOBAL
3% US
26% CANADA

Over 300,000
100,000 – 299,999
20,000 – 199,999
10,000 – 19,999
3,000 – 9,999
1,000 – 2,999
200 – 999
10 – 199
Below 10
No Data

LARGEST HYDROELECTRIC STATIONS WORLDWIDE CAPACITY (IN MW)

THREE GORGES DAM, CHINA — 22,500

ITAIPU DAM, BRAZIL/PARAGUAY — 14,000

GURI DAM, VENEZUELA — 8,850

TUCURUÍ DAM, BRAZIL — 8,370

GRAND COULEE DAM, WASHINGTON STATE, US — 6,809

People who live around hydro dams are sometimes forced to move because of flooding. Dams have displaced 40 to 80 million people worldwide.

PROS

- ✔ No greenhouse gases
- ✔ Low operating and maintenance costs
- ✔ Renewable source of energy
- ✔ Power plants can last for up to 100 years
- ✔ Domestic energy source in US and Canada
- ✔ Tidal and wave energy have large potential

CONS

- ✘ Dams can harm ecosystems, cause flooding, and increase earthquake risk
- ✘ Dam failure is rare but can be catastrophic
- ✘ Supply is affected by droughts and weather
- ✘ Plants are expensive and take a long time to build
- ✘ Site-specific: can only be built in certain places
- ✘ Dams can displace people who live nearby

GEOTHERMAL

WHAT IS IT?

Steam and hot water from deep within the earth are used to produce electricity or to heat buildings.

WHERE DOES GEOTHERMAL ENERGY COME FROM?

Deep inside the earth, radioactive particles are constantly decaying and producing heat.

Magma—super-hot melted rock—surrounds the earth's core.

Closer to the earth's surface, underground water and rock absorb heat from the magma.

In places near the borders of earth's plates—like the western part of the US, and Hawaii—some of that heat rises to the surface.

Volcanoes, hot springs, and geysers all come from the earth's geothermal energy bubbling up to the surface through cracks in tectonic plates.

HOW DOES GEOTHERMAL ELECTRICITY WORK?

1. Wells are dug into the earth, about 1.5–3 km (1–2 miles) deep.
2. Hot water and steam from reservoirs deep underground are brought up to the surface through pipes.
3. Inside the power plant, the steam spins a turbine and a generator converts that energy to produce electricity.
4. The steam cools and condenses into water, and is then injected back into the ground to be used again.

If we could find a way to access it all, there's enough geothermal energy in the earth to supply the whole planet's energy needs!

In Iceland,

26%

of all electricity is produced with geothermal power.

ENERGY FROM GEOTHERMAL

0.4%	0.2%	0%
GLOBAL	US	CANADA

GEOTHERMAL HEAT PUMPS

Geothermal energy can be used directly to heat and cool homes and other buildings. At the earth's surface, temperatures change a lot depending on the season and time of day. But about 3 meters (10 ft) below the surface, the underground temperature stays pretty much the same year-round. Geothermal systems pump hot water from underground to heat homes and buildings in the winter. In the summer, the pumps transfer heat from the air underground, cooling the building when it's hot.

Geothermal energy has been used for thousands of years; ancient Native Americans, Chinese, and Romans all used hot springs for bathing, heat, and cooking.

There are new ways to produce "enhanced" geothermal energy in places without underground reservoirs. Cold water is pumped underground to make cracks in hot, dry rock. As the water flows into the cracks, it's heated. Then it's pumped back above ground to be used for electricity generation.

PROS

- Produces very little GHG and no waste
- No fuel, mining, or transportation required
- Not intermittent like wind or solar energy
- Almost unlimited supply in US and Canada
- Enhanced geothermal energy has large potential

CONS

- Emits some sulfur dioxide
- Uses water and can affect water supply
- High construction costs for geothermal plants
- Can currently be used only in geothermal "hot spots"
- Technology for enhanced geothermal is still in development

BIOMASS AND BIOFUELS

WHAT IS IT?

Biomass is any organic matter from plants and animals (like wood, food crops, manure, or even garbage) used to produce energy. It can be burned to produce heat and generate electricity, or turned into a liquid (biofuel) that can power vehicles.

Burning biomass—like wood or grass—is one of the earliest ways humans used energy. Biomass is still the only fuel source for homes in many developing countries.

CARBON IN, CARBON OUT

The CO_2 created by burning biomass is eventually absorbed by the next harvest of trees and plants, as long as enough are replanted.

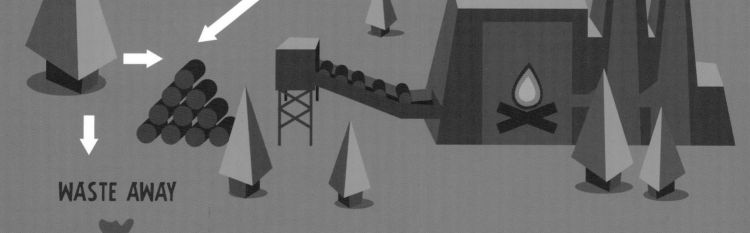

WASTE AWAY

1.9 kg
(4.4 lb)

Amount of garbage the average American throws away every day

Burning garbage to produce energy is a way of dealing with the amount of waste North Americans produce. It can reduce the volume of garbage we put into landfills by about 87 percent.

BIOFUELS

So-called first-generation biofuels turn food for humans into fuel for cars. This is an inefficient use of food, and drives up the price of crops like corn in countries where people rely on them as a staple. Second-generation biofuels made from products like used cooking oil, waste paper, or inedible parts of plants are a promising alternative.

10% GLOBAL   5% US   5% CANADA

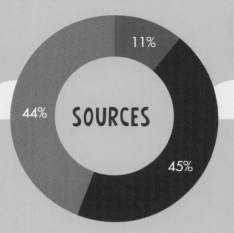

SOURCES
11%
44%
45%

 Biofuels, like ethanol or biodiesel, can be produced from rotting garbage, leftover cooking oils, or fermented crops like corn or sugarcane.

 Wood and **wood waste** (like bark, dead trees, and branches) are burned by industries to generate electricity, or in homes for heat and cooking.

 Household **garbage**, food scraps, yard clippings, and even some plastics can be burned in "waste-to-energy" plants to make steam and electricity.

8 bushels of corn is equivalent to: **82** liters (22 gallons) of ethonol fuel   **1** year of food for 1 person

Each year, 5 billion bushels of corn are turned into ethanol. These bushels contain enough calories to feed 412 million people all year.

For every **10** ears of corn grown in the US: **2** are consumed by humans   **4** are used for animal feed   **4** are used for ethanol production

PROS
- ✔ Can be domestically produced
- ✔ Lots of supply and widely available
- ✔ Low cost
- ✔ Cleaner than fossil fuels
- ✔ Helps deal with waste

CONS
- ✘ Requires water and land to grow
- ✘ Inefficient source of electricity
- ✘ Biofuels take lots of energy to produce and refine
- ✘ First-generation biofuels increase food costs
- ✘ Harvesting and transporting produces CO_2

NEW ENERGY SOURCES

HYDROGEN

WHAT IS IT?

Hydrogen is the most plentiful element in the universe, and it could be how the car of the future is powered. Hydrogen fuel cells use a chemical reaction between hydrogen and oxygen to generate electricity. The only byproducts are heat and water—no exhaust or GHGs.

WHERE IT'S AT:

As of 2014 there are test versions of fuel cell vehicles, but none are available to buy. It will be expensive to set up stations along roads and highways for refueling "H-cars." Problems with delivering and storing hydrogen—a highly flammable gas—must also be sorted out.

H₂

EFFICIENCY COMPARISON

20%
Car powered by gas

64%
Car powered by hydrogen fuel cells

100+:
number of hydrogen fuel cell buses in use around the world

$100,000:
what an H-car would cost if you bought one in 2014

$500 billion:
estimated amount to set up stations for H-car refueling in the US

Many people are working today to develop effective, environmentally friendly forms of energy that will help replace fossil fuels and reduce greenhouse gas emissions. New developments in "clean" energy are happening all the time. Let's explore some of the most promising.

ALGAE BIOFUEL

WHAT IS IT?

Biofuel can be created from algae, which is 50 percent oil. Algae is a good biofuel alternative to corn or other plants because it produces more oil using a smaller area than plants that grow on land, like corn. It produces hardly any waste, and it can be grown indoors.

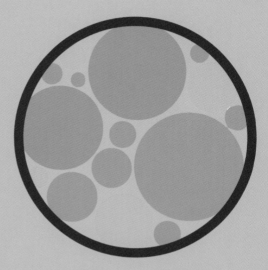

WHERE IT'S AT:

Research is ongoing, but it will take at least a few years before anyone's filling their tank with algae.

Algae actually cleans the air of greenhouse gases: it takes in CO_2 and replaces it with oxygen.

SAVING LAND

Algae can produce 10 times more oil (by area) than land plants like corn. To produce enough biofuel to replace all the world's fossil fuels it would take an area of land:

 about the size of Japan

ALGAE

 about the size of India

CORN

THORIUM

WHAT IS IT?

A radioactive element that can be used in nuclear reactors, thorium is a good alternative to traditional nuclear fuel—uranium—because it generates more energy with less waste. Unlike uranium, thorium actually burns up its own waste when it's used. It can even be mixed with waste from conventional nuclear plants, recycling dangerous nuclear waste into energy-producing fuel.

WHERE IT'S AT:

India and China are both developing thorium reactors, but converting the fuel into a usable form is still time-consuming and expensive.

COMPARISON OF THORIUM AND URANIUM REACTORS

To produce 1 gigawatt (1 billion watts) of electricity, it takes:

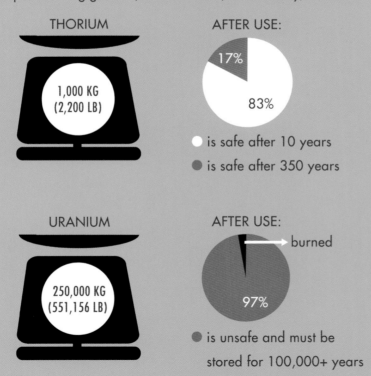

THORIUM

1,000 KG (2,200 LB)

AFTER USE:

17%

83%

○ is safe after 10 years
● is safe after 350 years

URANIUM

250,000 KG (551,156 LB)

AFTER USE:

→ burned

97%

● is unsafe and must be stored for 100,000+ years

By 2050, India plans to get 30 percent of its energy from thorium reactors.

OCEAN THERMAL ENERGY CONVERSION (OTEC)

WHAT IS IT?

Warm water from the ocean's surface is used to heat a low-boiling-point fluid like ammonia, which, as it vaporizes and expands, rotates a turbine to generate electricity. Then cold water from below is piped up to cool the vapor back into a liquid so it can be reused.

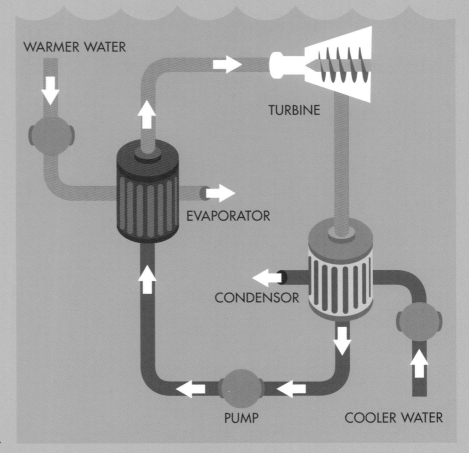

WHERE IT'S AT:

OTEC works best in tropical areas where there's a big temperature difference between surface and deeper water. There's one plant operating in Japan and several more in development, including plants off the coasts of Hawaii and China.

TIDAL POWER

Tidal power is another way to get energy from the ocean. It uses the motion of the ocean's tides, which are caused by gravity as the moon and earth spin, to rotate turbines and generate electricity. As of 2014 there are a few working tidal power stations, including ones off the coasts of France, South Korea, Nova Scotia, and Vancouver Island, with more stations planned.

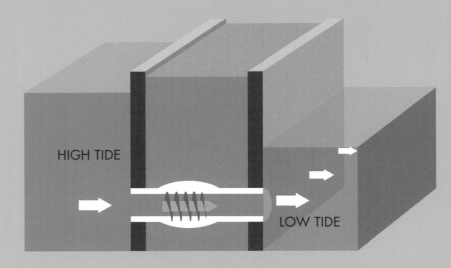

GLOBAL DEMAND

Humans use a lot more energy now than we did in the past. Today, we have all sorts of energy-consuming machines and appliances that we didn't have a century or two ago, like computers, phones, and cars. As the global population keeps growing, and more people around the world depend on driving vehicles and using electricity, our energy needs will continue to increase.

ESTIMATED DAILY ENERGY USE PER PERSON, BY TYPE OF SOCIETY
(IN 1,000 KILOCALORIES)

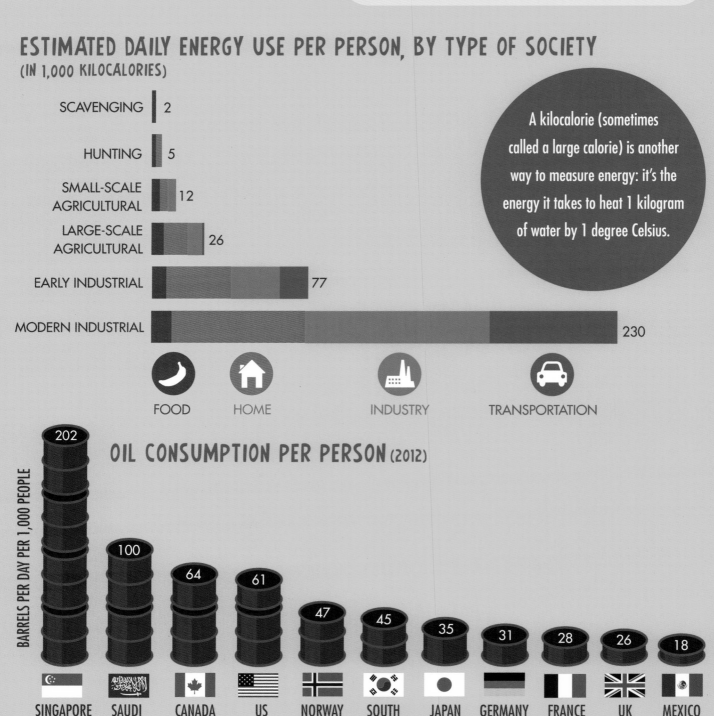

SCAVENGING — 2

HUNTING — 5

SMALL-SCALE AGRICULTURAL — 12

LARGE-SCALE AGRICULTURAL — 26

EARLY INDUSTRIAL — 77

MODERN INDUSTRIAL — 230

FOOD   HOME   INDUSTRY   TRANSPORTATION

A kilocalorie (sometimes called a large calorie) is another way to measure energy: it's the energy it takes to heat 1 kilogram of water by 1 degree Celsius.

OIL CONSUMPTION PER PERSON (2012)

BARRELS PER DAY PER 1,000 PEOPLE

SINGAPORE	SAUDI ARABIA	CANADA	US	NORWAY	SOUTH KOREA	JAPAN	GERMANY	FRANCE	UK	MEXICO
202	100	64	61	47	45	35	31	28	26	18

43

ENERGY USE BY COUNTRY

WORLD ENERGY
CONSUMPTION
PER PERSON

(in kg of oil equivalent)

OVER 10,000
5,001 – 10,000
2,501 – 5,000
1,001 – 2,500
501 – 1,000
0 – 500
NO DATA

GLOBAL ENERGY TODAY

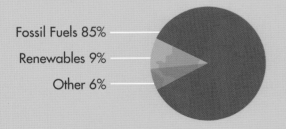

Fossil Fuels 85%

Renewables 9%

Other 6%

Experts say to avoid the worst effects of climate change, the energy picture should look more like this:

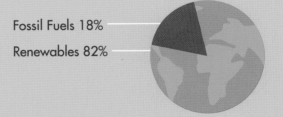

Fossil Fuels 18%

Renewables 82%

IF EVERYONE IN THE WORLD USED THE SAME AMOUNTS OF ENERGY AS NORTH AMERICANS, WE'D NEED:

5 times our world energy use today

16 times our world energy use by 2050

ENERGY AT HOME

HOW MUCH POWER DO YOUR HOUSEHOLD APPLIANCES USE?

 POWER USED (IN WATTS)

ANNUAL ENERGY CONSUMED
(EQUIVALENT IN LITERS/GALLONS OF GAS)

 **ELECTRIC FURNACE**
17,221
863/228

 **HAIR DRYER**
1,800
26/7

 **CENTRAL AIR-CONDITIONER**
5,000
1,507/398

 **MICROWAVE**
1,538
26/7

 **CLOTHES DRYER**
3,400
303/80

 **TOASTER**
1,100
11/3

 **OVEN**
2,300
254/67

 **ROOM AIR-CONDITIONER**
1,000
227/60

 **DISHWASHER**
1,800
204/54

 **WATER HEATER**
479
1,264/334

Think about everything in your house that uses energy. In a typical North American home, even if you don't have the TV on or a hair dryer running, energy is being used for all sorts of things you can't see: heating and air-conditioning rooms, keeping the fridge cold, and sending electricity to plugged-in devices.

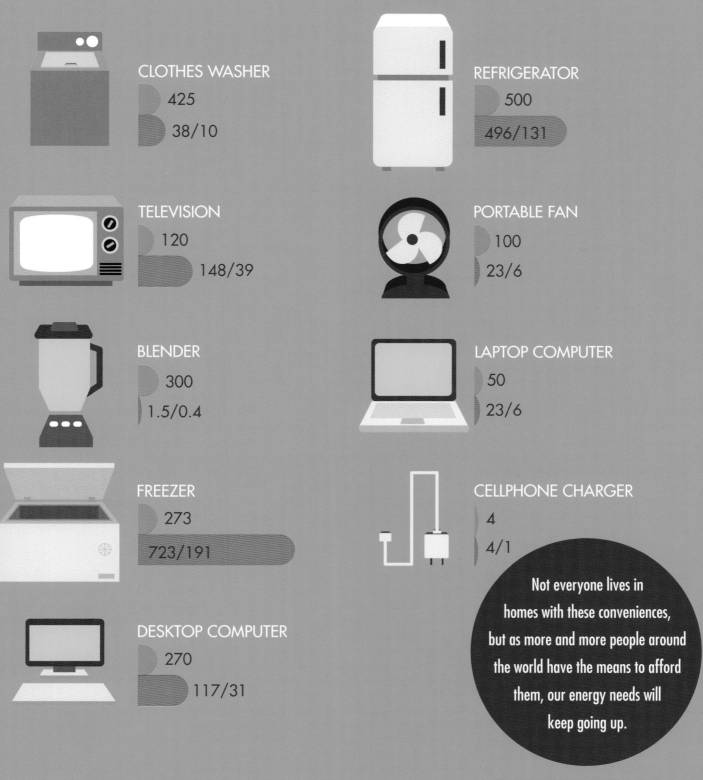

CLOTHES WASHER
425
38/10

REFRIGERATOR
500
496/131

TELEVISION
120
148/39

PORTABLE FAN
100
23/6

BLENDER
300
1.5/0.4

LAPTOP COMPUTER
50
23/6

FREEZER
273
723/191

CELLPHONE CHARGER
4
4/1

DESKTOP COMPUTER
270
117/31

Not everyone lives in homes with these conveniences, but as more and more people around the world have the means to afford them, our energy needs will keep going up.

ENERGY EFFICIENCY

10% LIGHT

90% HEAT

We use light bulbs to provide light, but traditional incandescent bulbs (which have a wire inside that glows when an electric current passes through it) lose most of their energy through heat.

The average house uses **32 light bulbs**, including ones inside fridges and ovens.

Newer types of light bulbs are more efficient than incandescent bulbs. Compact fluorescent light bulbs (CFLs) have a spiral tube with mercury gas inside, and produce light when electricity makes the gas molecules move. LED lights, which are even more efficient, are used in everything from digital watches to traffic lights.

LIGHT BULB COMPARISON CHART

TYPE	AVG. PRICE	WATTAGE	LIFESPAN HRS	ENERGY COST/10,000 HRS
INCANDESCENT	$	60	1,000	$$$$$ $$$$$
CFL	$$$$	15	8,000	$$$$$
LED	$$$$$ $$$$$	10	50,000	$$

One big way to save energy is to make sure we use it efficiently. Modern appliances—like washing machines and fridges—do their jobs using much less energy than older appliances. But there are still ways to reduce the amount of energy we waste.

Computer use around the world has gone way up since 2001. The massive server farms and cell towers that keep us connected use up a lot of energy too. Worldwide, there are now:

250 MILLION LAPTOPS

1 BILLION SMARTPHONES

100 MILLION SERVERS

VAMPIRE POWER

Electric devices use power whenever they're plugged in, even if they're turned off. It's called vampire power. Appliances like TVs and microwaves use up to half as much power on standby mode as when they're in use. Over their lifetimes, they can actually use more power when they're off than when they're warming up your dinner or playing your favorite show!

$3 BILLION The amount vampire power costs consumers in the US per year.

10% The amount of all household electricity wasted due to vampire power.

> The vampire power wasted in the US each year is equivalent to the annual electricity use of Italy!

HOW CAN YOU SAVE ENERGY?

AT HOME

Reduce, reuse, and recycle everything you can.

Turn off the lights when no one is in the room, and encourage your parents to buy LED lights.

Take shorter showers, and use cool water instead of hot to wash your hands.

Become your family's official drip-checker: Leaky faucets and showerheads waste a lot of energy. Let your parents know if you spot a dripping tap.

Unplug cellphones and computers when they're done charging, and shut them off overnight. Before you go away on holidays, unplug TV sets, game consoles, stereos, and clocks.

AT SCHOOL

Start an eco club or a recycling program with friends.

Plant trees or a small garden on your school grounds.

Organize a "litterless lunch" or "walk to school" **challenge for a week**.

Talk to a teacher or principal about getting the whole school involved in a "green challenge."

Can your school reduce the amount of energy it uses? You could even start a friendly competition with a nearby school to see who can reduce energy use more.

Energy is something we all need to think about. Our choices about how much we use, and in which forms, have repercussions for everyone in the world. A big part of the energy used worldwide comes from everyday activities and choices made by ordinary people. There are lots of things you can do to make a positive energy impact, whether it's in your own home, at school, or in the wider world.

YOUR COMMUNITY

If you're not going far, **bike, walk, or take the bus** instead of asking your parents for a ride.

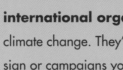

Look for games, gadgets, or clothes at garage sales or secondhand shops, or else trade with friends—that saves the energy of making and transporting new things.

Write a letter to your local paper or community newsletter **explaining something kids can do to save energy,** like walking to school one day a week.

Go online and find out if there are any interesting energy projects in your state or province, like a solar power farm or geothermal plant. Write to your congressperson or MP to encourage them to support the program.

energy projects 🔍

THE GLOBE

Use social media to follow environmental groups and international organizations concerned about energy and climate change. They'll keep you informed about petitions you can sign or campaigns you can get involved with.

Follow news on the Internet about energy and climate issues around the world. You could do a school project about an innovative energy program in another country, or about how climate change is affecting people in developing regions.

Help raise money or awareness for an energy-positive cause, like a program that provides solar or hydroelectric power to people in impoverished areas.

ENERGY TERMS

There are various ways to measure energy. Here are some that are used in this book.

watt (W): A watt is a unit that measures an amount of power (the speed at which energy flows). Household appliances show a watt rating, which tells you how quickly energy must be generated to run the device. A typical light bulb needs 40 to 100 watts of power.

kilowatt (kW) = one thousand watts. Power for engines, motors, and heaters is normally measured in kW.

megawatt (MW) = one million watts. Large ships, trains, and machines, nuclear power plants, and server farms measure their output in MW.

gigawatt (GW) = one billion watts. A large power plant can produce over 1 GW of power.

terawatt (TW) = one trillion watts. The average power used by all the people on earth in 2013 was around 17 TW.

A **watt-hour** is a unit of energy measured by calculating the power in watts used over an hour. For instance, a light bulb with a power rating of 100 W left on for an hour uses 100 watt-hours (W·h) of energy. Energy used by households is usually measured in kilowatt-hours (kWh), while larger amounts are measured in terawatt-hours (TWh).

SELECTED SOURCES

All online sources retrieved May 2014

Bishop, Amanda. *Energy Conservation.* New York: Cavendish Square Publishing, 2008.

DeGunther, Rik. *Alternative Energy for Dummies.* Hoboken, N.J.: Wiley Publishing, 2009.

Dukes, Jeffrey S. "Burning Buried Sunshine: Human Consumption of Ancient Solar Energy." *Climatic Change* 61 (Nov. 2003): 1–2, pp 31–44. doi: 10.1023/A:1026391317686.

General Electric Company. "The amazing road to your home." ge-flexibility.com/power-generation-basics/how-electricity-is-produced/index.html

Goldemberg, José. *Energy: What Everyone Needs to Know.* New York: Oxford University Press, 2012.

Hughes, David. "Drill, Baby, Drill." Post Carbon Institute (website), Feb. 2013. postcarbon.org/drill-baby-drill/

(Selected Sources continued)

Johnson, Keith. "Is Nuclear Power Renewable Energy?" Environmental Capital (blog), *Wall Street Journal*, May 21, 2009. blogs.wsj.com/environmentalcapital/2009/05/21/is-nuclear-power-renewable-energy/

Knight, M.J. *Why Should I Switch Off the Light?* Mankato, MN: Black Rabbit Books, 2009.

Landau, Elaine. *The History of Energy.* Minneapolis: Twenty-First Century Books, 2006.

Lanz, Helen. *Go Green: Having the Energy.* North Mankato, MN: Sea-to-Sea Publications, 2012.

Nuwer, Rachel. "Oil Sands Mining Uses Up Almost as Much Energy as It Produces." *Inside Climate News*, Feb. 19, 2013. insideclimate-news.org/news/20130219/oil-sands-mining-tar-sands-alberta-canada-energy-return-on-investment-eroi-natural-gas-in-situ-dilbit-bitumen

Preemptive Media for AIR. "The Fossil Fuel Fix" (infographic). 2006. pm-air.net/images/PMair_map.jpg

Reilly, Kathleen M. *Energy: 25 Projects Investigate Why We Need Power and How We Get It.* White River Junction, VT: Nomad Press, 2009.

Union of Concerned Scientists. "A Short History of Energy." ucsusa.org/clean_energy/our-energy-choices/a-short-history-of-energy.html

Statistics taken from the following websites

Canadian Electricity Association, Power for the Future website. "Data World." powerforthefuture.ca/data-world/

Enerdata. "Global Energy Statistical Yearbook 2013." yearbook.ener-data.net/

Environment Canada. "Energy Production." ec.gc.ca/energie-energy/

Food or Fuel? foodorfuel.weebly.com/

International Energy Agency. iea.org

National Academies. "What You Need to Know About Energy." needtoknow.nas.edu/energy/

Natural Resources Canada. "Energy." nrcan.gc.ca/energy

United States Environmental Protection Agency. "Overview of Greenhouse Gases." epa.gov/climatechange/ghgemissions/gases.html

US Department of Energy. energy.gov

US Energy Information Administration. eia.gov

US Energy Information Administration. "Energy Kids." eia.gov/kids/index.cfm

Note to readers:
The statistics used in this book are drawn from the latest information available at press time. Because numbers and percentages have sometimes been rounded, totals may not add up to 100 percent. In cases where numbers may vary (e.g., for power ratings of appliances), averages have been used.

INDEX

Look for these other great books from Annick Press:

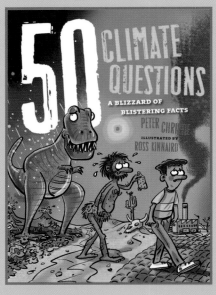

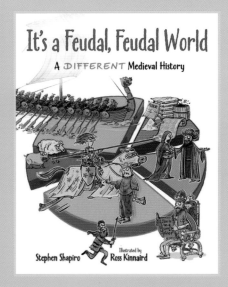

Native Americans:
A Visual Exploration
by S.N. Paleja
paperback $12.95 | hardcover $19.95

*White Ravens Collection,
International Youth Library, Munich

"An excellent introduction to indigenous peoples throughout the United States and Canada and a great jumping off point to further exploration ..."—*Resource Links*

"The colorful pictures help to draw children's interest and they also help reluctant readers access the content."—*The Deakin Review of Children's Literature*

"... may ultimately be the best thing out on the market today."—*School Library Journal.com*

"A wonderful introduction to American Indians. This engaging book serves as a great starting point for social studies investigations."—*Teacher Librarian*

50 Climate Questions:
A Blizzard of Blistering Facts
50 Questions series
by Peter Christie
illustrated by Ross Kinnaird
paperback $14.95 | hardcover $22.95

*Best Books for Kids & Teens,
Canadian Children's Book Centre

*Recommended Reads List,
Canadian Toy Testing Council

"History + meteorology = hilarity in this heavily illustrated, nicely designed jaunt through four billion years of Earth's history."
—*School Library Journal*

"Gives young readers a quick overview of the many ways in which climate has changed the world and the creatures living on it ..."—*Booklist*

"A humorous, appealing, and informative look at climate change that can be enjoyed whether one is looking for a recreational read or for information for a school project."
—*CM Reviews*

It's a Feudal, Feudal World:
A Different Medieval History
by Stephen Shapiro
illustrated by Ross Kinnaird
paperback $14.95 | hardcover $24.95

*Best Books for Kids & Teens 2014,
Canadian Children's Book Centre

*2014 Next Generation Indie Book
Award finalist

*Silver Birch Award nomination,
Ontario Library Association

"This very appealing graphic text is truly a 'different' history of the Middle Ages! ... Each page contains a wealth of clearly presented information."
—*Resource Links*

"Gets below the surface on more than one occasion ... likely to encourage readers to take the next step in learning about medieval times."
—*Kirkus Reviews*

"A creative and useful book that will be an added treasure to any school library or classroom. Highly recommended."—*CM Reviews*